YAARI VE

LET'S CELEBRATE FRIENDSHIP

TARANDEEP KAUR BHASIN

Copyright © Tarandeep Kaur Bhasin
All Rights Reserved.

This book is dedicated to nine of my most dear friends. They make my life cheerful, always! All of them have helped me in unique ways to evolve and become a better version of myself.

Contents

Preface

Since time immemorial, humans have formed associations with fellow humans. Man is a social being and cannot live in isolation.

We come across many people every day. Only a handful of those remains with us lifelong.

As the adage goes, "You are known by the kind of company you keep."

Good friends are like a blessing. They help you evolve. They help you to become the best version of yourself.

Like in every relationship, friendship also has ups and downs. What matters is the willingness to sustain the relationship.

This little book is an endeavour to celebrate friendship. It contains about 9 of my bosom friends. Life will be colourless without them. Each of them adds value to my life. One is a doctor whereas the other is a lawyer. All of these friends are from different walks of life.

The distance at times may separate us. We may not talk too often. However, the bond of the heart binds us together.

Through this book, I want to make each of my close friends feel special.

CHAPTER ONE

The Enlivening Pal- Ms. Ranjit Batra

Ms. Ranjit Batra

Testing times are undoubtedly harsh, but they reveal to us our well-wishers. Fair-weather friends exist in every nook and corner. After all, who doesn't like partying around and celebrating when times are rosy? But how many stand by you, wiping your tears? In a challenging world, great buddies make life worth living.

Man is a social being and cannot exist in isolation. Socializing is a primitive need for humans. Our company decides to a large extent what we become.

Ms. Ranjit Batra, a retired convent school teacher is one of my best pals. She has a very rich experience in the teaching industry. She is the force behind shaping the lives of thousands of young children. The ease with which she interacts with me makes her one of my best friends. There is much to learn from her life and teaching experiences.

My maternal grandmother told me that Ms. Batra held me in her arms when I was an infant. Our association has been for more than two decades.

Life is never a bed of roses for anyone. Highs and lows are an integral part of our daily life. One should never forget the gesture shown by fellow human beings during hours of sorrow. Ms. Batra supported our family at such an hour.

Life is a roller coaster ride. Painful situations pass, however, the people who stand by you in such testing situations should be remembered.

When I was very ill, Ms. Batra was the one who made it a point to regularly send me a good morning message. The feelings attached to the good morning wishes were so positive that they never failed to make me smile.

I am hale and hearty now, but I will never forget the efforts of Ms. Batra. Both of us still exchange good morning wishes daily. I believe it is the perfect start for each new day.

Having a magnanimous heart, Ms. Batra is always willing to help others selflessly. An altruistic attitude like hers is hard to find in today's materialistic world.

It is a pleasure to know you, Ms. Batra. I pray that God fills your life with joy, always!

The Gregarious Friend-
Mrs. Mamta Praveen

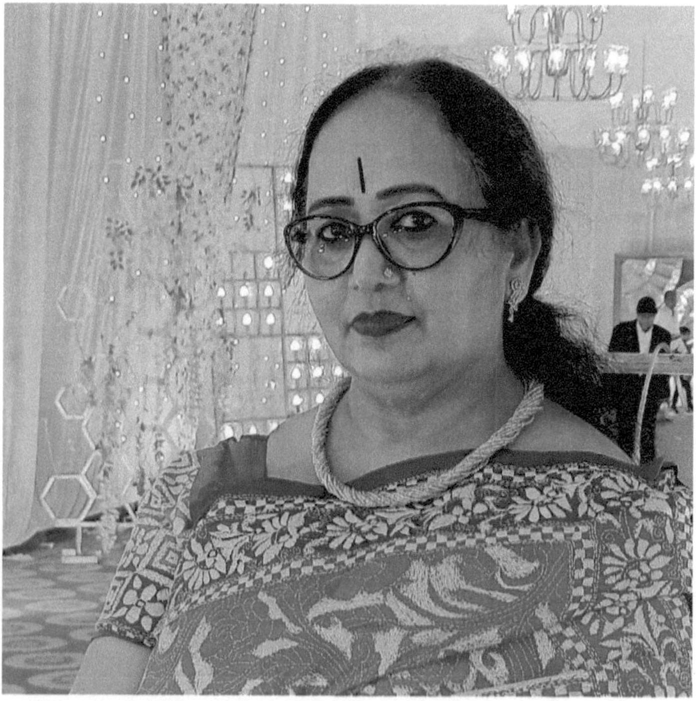

Mrs. Mamta Praveen

Teaching has always been my passion. How a teacher moulds the character of a student fascinates me. Teaching might look simple, but it is the toughest of all professions. Talk about a doctor, lawyer, or a professional from any field; behind each is a hardworking teacher. We are nothing without our teachers!

In 2018, I was lucky to get a job as a primary school teacher in a reputed school. With opportunities come challenges. Handling primary children is not a cakewalk.

I was nervous about how I will manage all the kids on my own. Then the almighty sent Mrs. Mamta to my rescue. Indeed, she was a respite! Mrs. Mamta happened to be a very senior co-colleague of mine. With a rich experience of more than a decade, the simplicity with which Mrs. Mamta approached me took me by surprise. She offered me help and said that she would be visiting my class during recess so that I could have my lunch. She promised to look after the students in my class. She not only verbally offered help but used to visit my class every day.

Whenever I found myself in troubled waters, I found Mrs. Mamta standing beside me like a pillar of support.

She loved me like her daughter. She used to advise me on various topics. Sometimes scolding, sometimes appreciating, my experience in that school was made memorable by this sweet friend of mine.

Mrs. Mamta is a fantastic Hindi teacher whom children love. She is also a great dancer and theatre artist.

Mrs. Mamta is a source of immense creativity. She has acted and supervised various plays and dramas. Despite all these laurels in her kitty, she is a very down-to-earth human being.

She knows my taste well and always gifts me jewellery items- because they never fail to bring a smile to my face!

Mrs. Mamta, I love you. You are a blessing that I cherish from the core of my heart.

The Sparkling Buddy– Mrs. Roli Pandey

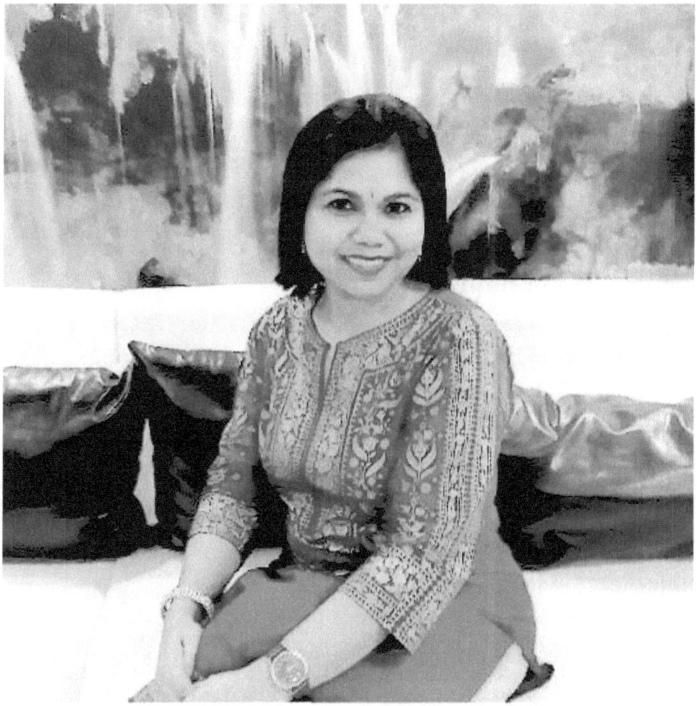

Mrs. Roli Pandey

In the professional sphere, one comes across a plethora of people. As work is the top priority, one hardly gets time to deepen relationships on a personal level. Even when one does, how long the bond sustains is the question. Professional jealousy and a host of other factors amount to a lack of forming bonds that sustain.

While working as a Special Educator in one of the reputed schools, I came across Mrs. Roli. She happened to be a Mathematics teacher there.

The common thing between us was the Bachelor of Education course. Two of us were in the same semester but at different colleges.

One day, we found out while conversing that we were stuck with the same practical part of our 3rd semester. As we were sailing in the same boat, we could easily relate to each other's agony.

We tried to boost each other's morale. Together we decided to talk to our university authorities and find out a solution to our problem.

In the process, I ended up staying at Mrs. Roli's house for a night as the next day was our practical exam. We studied together, laughed, and enjoyed the time. The tension subsided because we two were together on our journey.

Mrs. Roli draped me in a *saree* thenext day. We successfully gave our exam. Bachelor of Education got completed with flying colours in 2020.

The bond between us grew so strong that despite Mrs. Roli being a senior co-colleague, we often spent hours talking together. Ranging from spirituality to the tinsel town gossip, we can discuss anything under the sun when we are together.

Mrs. Roli is a very broad-minded lady. She is non-judgmental and is a keen observer and listener. She is always willing to grow and learn from her surroundings. Whenever anyone approaches her for help, she always welcomes the individual with an open arm.

A calculative subject like Math is also made very interesting for the students by her. They love her class.

Not only a great teacher and friend, but Mrs. Roli is also a loving wife and mother. Her way of balancing all her roles is commendable!

Certain stressful conditions are a blessing in disguise, just like the Bachelor of Education practical exam.

I feel very fortunate to have come across such a gem of a person like Mrs. Roli. May you succeed in all your endeavours, my dear friend.

The Happy go Lucky Pal- Dr. Smita Srivastava

Dr. Smita Srivastava

I decided to take Psychology directly in my Post Graduation. I hardly knew the subject. It seemed fascinating to me. I thought I would be able to help others and myself learn about the human psyche.

So, I enrolled myself at IGNOU University for a distance learning course- a master's in Psychology. I had never done a distance learning degree before this. So, I was unaware of the upcoming challenges.

There was an internship in our 2nd year. Since I was doing a job, I couldn't do an internship in the morning.

My mother knew Dr. Smita. She said I could request her for the internship under her guidance.

I was a little hesitant to visit and talk to Dr. Smita. She is a renowned psychiatrist.

Contrary to my expectations, Dr. Smita agreed to the internship under her. She even allowed me to interact with her patients and take notes of their symptoms. While the patients used to wait for their turn, I used to interact with them. Later I used to discuss the symptoms with Dr. Smita.

Interacting with her patients helped me to gain a realistic view of the psychiatric problems.

Dr. Smita is actively involved in writing articles and talk shows related to mental health issues. Generally, people are unwilling to go to a psychiatrist because of the stigma attached to mental health issues. However, while doing my internship under Dr. Smita, I found that the ambiance had positivity. Dr. Smita always gives sufficient time to all her patients. She has a smile on her face.

Though my master's in Psychology is over, I still interact with Dr. Smita. We exchange good morning wishes very often. Interacting with her always makes me happy.

Wish you all the very best Dr. Smita. May God bless you. You are not only a great doctor but a great human too.

The Oldest Friend- Pushkal Singh

Pushkal Singh

Looks are deceptive! The surface visible is just the tip of the iceberg. Many unknown facets get hidden underneath.

Pushkal, my oldest school friend, has always warned me to judge people carefully. She is a mature girl and takes her own sweet time before coming to any conclusion. As the adage goes, "Haste makes waste"; Pushkal takes a holistic view before concluding.

Pushkal is a medical student. She is very focused. Her dressing sense is simple yet elegant. Simple, pastel colours are what she likes.

Pushkal kept my nickname as "Tommy". Since my school days, she has been calling me by this name. The name has been so popular that even her family members call me by this name. Pushkal's mother is a gem of a person. I have rarely seen people like her. She loves me a lot. She always encourages me to give my best.

Pushkal and I met in class 1. Yes, the friendship is that old. There were years in between when we weren't in touch.

Suddenly, one day I got a message from Pushkal. Then a new chapter of our friendship began. Now, I believe that with each passing day, our bond grows stronger.

I can never forget the help rendered by Pushkal when I was in great trouble. It was Covid times. I didn't know which doctor to approach. I was in search of a good gynaecologist. I just discussed the matter with Pushkal as she is a medical student. She immediately provided me with a gynaecologist contact whom she knew well.

Had Pushkal not come to my rescue, I would not have recovered so fast. She even offered to go to the gynaecologist with me, despite knowing I had corona-like symptoms.

Pushkal has always motivated me in all my endeavours. Be it a writing venture or a video-making one, she has always been very encouraging.

I pray that Pushkal becomes a good doctor soon. May she get all the happiness that she deserves!

The Empathetic Companion- Shipra Das

Shipra Das

Adolescence is a period of great emotional upheaval. On the one hand, there is enormous pressure to prove your mettle. On the other, the dancing hormone levels bring behavioural changes. It becomes more challenging if there is a change in school and friends.

I had to change my school after grade 10th. I was fortunate to get admission is one of the oldest and most reputed convent schools in the city. Though everything seemed very pleasant initially, I was completely unaware of the challenges waiting for me.

New school, new teachers, and new classmates. I found myself lost. It was hard for me to adjust to the new surroundings.

Accidently, one day while rehearsing for the annual function practice, I came across my now bosom friend, Shipra Das. Both of us met through a common friend of ours.

We began conversing. We enjoyed each other's company so much that it seemed as if we knew each other already.

Since Shipra was in the Humanities section and I was in the commerce section, we decided to meet during recess each day.

Without fail, we started meeting each other daily. Those 20 minutes of recess were the most cherished moments in the entire day. My gloomy school life got painted with colours of happiness.

Since English was a common subject, I remember Shipra and me discussing Shakespeare's Macbeth whenever we got time. She even introduced me fondly to all her friends. It made me feel welcomed in the new school.

Our association in school was limited to just two years. School life ended but not our friendship. Shipra went to Bangalore to pursue her Law studies while I studied at Lucknow.

Though we were miles apart, our bond never weakened. Owing to time constraints, we couldn't talk very frequently. However, this didn't affect the feelings we had for each other.

Whenever Shipra visited Lucknow, we made it a point that we meet. The good old days' memories were revived, always.

We even went to the Golden Temple together in 2020. The memories of that beautiful trip will always be etched in my mind.

Where there is love, there is fight too! Shipra and I also fight. However, that deepens our bond in the end.

She is a very empathetic girl. She ensures that she makes her friends feel special, always! She is hardworking and faces all odds with a smile. No matter how difficult a situation pops up, she fights it bravely.

Shipra is the one I can always bank on. 1 A.M. or 1 P.M., it never makes a difference; she is always there to support me.

Shipra, I treasure our friendship. It is one of the dearest things to me. Just be my friend always!

CHAPTER SEVEN

The Congenial Buddy–Falguni Singh

Falguni Singh

Nature has always fascinated me. Natural beauty leaves me in awe. It is a delight to be among plants and animals. Also, it is good to be with those humans who share similar interests with you.

Falguni happens to be my childhood school friend. I remember she had a beautiful aquarium in her house that attracted me. Not only this, but her mother had also kept a well-maintained garden with a variety of plants.

Falguni's house is very near to mine. As kids, we used to play together and did cycling. Falguni's mother is also very welcoming.

Falguni is a reserved person. Though an introvert, once Falguni feels comfortable with someone, she gets along well.

I left the school in which we studied together after grade 10. I went to a convent school. I took the commerce stream while Falguni took science

.

We lost touch for years. One day suddenly Falguni came to meet me. I was taken aback because a lot many years had passed. There was no contact.

Although we met after a gap, there were many things to talk about. We had a great time since that day.

We have been meeting often since then. Both of us get excited whenever we plan to meet. There is always a range of topics to talk. We start with a topic and then hop to various other topics.

Falguni is a simple girl. I never have to think much about what to wear when we have to meet. I can just be myself. There are no filters needed. Such a type of ease is what makes a relationship sustain. You are what you are. The other person accepts you in the same way as you are.

Falguni is a sincere student. I have seen her studying diligently for competitive exams. She has always given her best when it comes to the career front.

I wish you the best of luck in your future, Falguni. The devotion with which you are proceeding in life will take you miles. Keep smiling always!

The Encouraging Friend- Pinky Varshney

Pinky Varshney

Life is all about celebrating the little moments of togetherness. At times we wait for huge events to happen. We think that we will celebrate when we get our degree or land a good job. We fail to realize that each day is a blessing.

The fact that you are alive is a reason to celebrate.

While pursuing my Bachelor of Education, I met Pinky.

In our B.Ed., we had to visit a school library as a part of our training. That was the first time when Pinky and I interacted with each other. Draped in *saree,* five of us went to a school for a library visit. We hardly knew each other.

Pinky has a very soothing voice. It is always a pleasure to talk to her. The smile on her face is so encouraging.

She is laborious and very studious. I still remember how well she used to make notes of everything for the exams. She is very good at painting too! Above everything, Pinky has a golden heart.

It has been only two-three years of knowing Pinky. However, she has made a great place in my heart. Her kind and compassionate nature are what attracts me the most.

I would love to deepen our bond further, Pinky. Keep making those beautiful paintings. I would be extremely happy to have one of those! Love you, dear.

The Zestful Buddy-Harpreet Kaur

Harpreet Kaur

"Hi. I guess you were my senior in Loreto Convent", said Harpreet. Well, that was our first interaction. Harpreet was sitting in the front seat. As soon as she saw me, she asked if I knew her as we had studied in the same school.

Like a zombie, I entered my Bachelor of Education classroom. The class was very boring. However, meeting and talking to Harpreet broke the monotony of the day.

Harpreet is tall and pretty. She likes cooking in her free time. I am a big foodie but I run away from cooking. Whenever Harpreet tells me about her cooking classes, it waters my mouth. I wish to learn cooking from her someday.

Bachelor of Education was a challenging course for me. Our professors hardly taught us, and I was also working. I consider myself fortunate enough to have come across Harpreet.

Especially during the fourth semester of Bachelor of Education, we became close friends. We used to discuss the theory subject over a call. Peer learning and group study have always been beneficial for me. Studying with Harpreet was a boon. The theory paper would have been a humungous task without Harpreet.

Now, our Bachelor of Education course is successfully over. However, we never fail to be in touch. Whenever Harpreet and I talk over a call, it exceeds at least an hour. There are so many topics to discuss. Practically everything under the sun, we discuss.

I like theology a lot. Harpreet is also very spiritual. So, at times we discuss God. Also, she loves my voice. She always praises the way I speak. It makes me feel great. She never fails to motivate me in whatever I try.

Individual differences make the world a beautiful place. Harpreet loves cooking while I love eating. There are some similarities and some dissimilarities between us. However, the factor which binds us together is the ability to listen to and respect each other's views. That's how life works. We may vary on different things with our friends, but we treasure the good traits rather than the bad ones.

Harpreet, keep up your spirit high as always! Wish to take some fitness tips from you. May you have a happy life ahead.

Picture Gallery

www.ingramcontent.com/pod-product-compliance
Lightning Source LLC
Chambersburg PA
CBHW021812150726
47989CB00004B/1896